Bakst

1866-1924

D1312993

Grange
BOOKS

Text: Elisabeth Ingles

Page 4:
Design for the costume of Nijinsky in the ballet
L'Après-Midi d'un faune, 1912
Watercolour, gouache and gold paint on paper mounted on
cardboard, 40 x 27 cm. Musée d'Orsay, Paris

Layout:
Baseline Co Ltd
127-129A Nguyen Hue
Fiditourist 3rd Floor
District 1, Ho Chi Minh City
Vietnam

© 2007, Sirrocco, London, UK
© 2007, Confidential Concepts, Worldwide, USA

Published in 2007 by Grange Books
an imprint of Grange Books Plc
The Grange Kingsnorth Industrial Estate
Hoo, nr Rochester, Kent ME3 9ND
www.grangebooks.co.uk

ISBN: 978-1-84013-853-5

Printed in China

Foreword

"A marvellously decorative artist with great taste, infinite imagination, extraordinarily refined and aristocratic."

— Bakst's friend and colleague Anna Ostroumova-Lebedeva.

4

Biography

1866: Leon Bakst (originally called Lev Samoilovich Rosenberg) was born on 9 May in Grodno (Belarus) into a middle-class Jewish family.

1883-1886: He attended the Imperial Academy of Fine Arts in St Petersburg but was expelled after displeasing the school authorities with his painting of *Madonna Weeping Over Christ* in which all the figures were Jewish.

From 1886: He started his artistic career as an illustrator for magazines.

1890: He met Alexandre Benois and with him travelled regularly through Europe where he came in contact with local artists. He studied in Paris with a number of notable artists including Jean-Léon Gérôme at the Académie Julian.

1896: He returned to St Petersburg and began to gain notoriety for his book designs and his portraits.

1898: He co-founded the group World of Art with Alexandre Benois and Serge Diaghilev (*Mir Iskusstva*).

1902-1903: He debuted with the stage design for the Hermitage and Alexandrinsky Theatres in St Petersburg. Afterwards, he received several commissions from the Mariinsky Theatre.

L . Bakst

1906:	He was invited to teach drawing at Yelizaveta Zvantseva's liberal school of painting, one of whose later students was Marc Chagall. He also went to Paris to prepare the Russian section of the annual art exhibition, the Salon d'Automne.
1909:	He again returned to France in 1908, where he began his collaboration with Sergei Diaghilev. This resulted in the founding of the Ballets Russes, where Bakst became the artistic director. His stage designs quickly brought him international fame.
1910s:	Bakst's brilliant and exotic creations influenced fashions in dress and interior decoration for many years to come. He was the principal artist to introduce Orientalism into fashion. Most notable are his costume designs for Diaghilev's *Shéhérazade* (1910) and *L'Après-Midi d'un faune* (1912).
1912:	He settled in Paris in 1912, after being exiled because of his Jewish origins.
1920:	The publisher of *Vogue Magazine*, Conde Nast, was after Bakst to persuade him to draw a cover for Vogue.
1924:	He died in Paris on 27 December, at the age of fifty-eight.

Introduction

B etween the 1870s and 1917, the whole way of life in Russia was undergoing a tremendous series of changes. A vast range of disparate factors contributed to the restlessness of the period, not only in cultural developments but in the political arena as well. The literature of the day both stimulated and reflected these currents of change. Dostoyevsky and Turgenev had much to say on the subject of social injustice.

Paris Welcoming Admiral Avelan

1893-1900
Oil on canvas
The Central Navy Museum, St Petersburg

Gorky embraced the growing revolutionary fervour of the turn of the century, and a prose poem written by him in 1901 provided a rallying-call for the reforming movement.

Ballet, which had developed in St Petersburg from 1738 as a consequence of Peter the Great's admiration for French and Italian culture and later took root in Moscow, remained one of the most popular artistic entertainments throughout the nineteenth century, achieving new heights of grandeur through the input of such choreographers as

Portrait of Valery Nuvel

1895
Watercolour on paper, mounted on cardboard, 57 x 44.2 cm
Russian Museum, St Petersburg

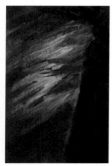

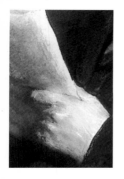

Marius Petipa (1822-1910) and composers such as Piotr Ilyich Tchaikovsky (1840-1893) – a partnership responsible for the three evergreen classics: *Swan Lake, The Sleeping Beauty* and *The Nutcracker*. Opera, too, was beginning to emerge from the obscurity in which it had languished earlier in the century. Nothing really innovative leapt out at the audience; little, except perhaps Tchaikovsky's operatic essay on the super-natural, *The Queen of Spades*, administered a shock to their sensibilities.

Portrait of Alexander Benois

1898
Watercolour and pastel on paper mounted on cardboard
64.5 x 110.3 cm
Russian Museum, St Petersburg

13

Diaghilev was to change all this. Somehow he had the vision to put together an infinite variety of widely divergent talents and see what happened. Diaghilev and his fellow-founders of *Mir Iskusstva* (the World of Art) drew into their orbit artists, musicians, dancers and singers whose names are today a byword for excitement, for colour and glamour, and for the shock value of a radical new approach to the arts.

Dolls Market

───────────

1899
Design for poster, pastel on cardboard, 72 x 98 cm
Russian Museum, St Petersburg

Diaghilev's Ballets Russes, the immediate offshoot of this artistic grouping, was to be the showcase for the genius of the painters Benois and Picasso as well as Bakst; the composers Ravel, de Falla, Debussy and Stravinsky; the choreographer Fokine and the dancers Pavlova, Karsavina and Nijinsky. Bakst fits effortlessly into this incomparable roll-call of stars.

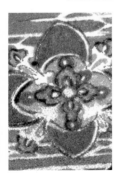

The Chinese Woman

c. 1900
Series of twelve postcards for the ballet *The Fairy Doll*
Editions de la commune Sainte Eglise

Лит А Иланна

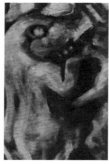

Formative Influences
Childhood, Youth and Early Career
1866-1890

Bakst came from a bourgeois Jewish family of comfortable means – his father was a successful businessman, his grandfather had earned a very good living as a tailor. The boy was born Lev Samuilovich Rosenberg on 9 May, 1866 in the town of Grodno, in what is now Belarus. The family moved to St Petersburg, then the Russian capital, when he was a few months old,

Siamese Sacred Dance

1901
The State Tretyakov Gallery, Moscow

and the northern city was to be his home town for nearly thirty years. As soon as he was old enough, Bakst was taken by his parents to the theatre, and drank in every detail of this wonderful world of make-believe. No doubt his childish "performances". At home were also fuelled by the plays he saw – certainly the home theatricals would have grown more polished and sophisticated.

Design for the costume of a huntress nymph in the ballet *Sylvia*

1901
Watercolour, pencil and bronze on paper, 28.1 x 21.1 cm
Russian Museum, St Petersburg

Obstinately, he insisted that he wanted to study art, and eventually his parents' opposition crumbled when they received advice from the sculptor Mark Antokolski, a leading figure among the Itinerants, that Lev was capable of producing work of top quality.

At the age of seventeen the young Bakst was enrolled at the Academy, an institution that was unfortunately already in decline and had little to offer the brightest talents of the day. He did not have unqualified success there – quite the opposite, in fact.

Set design for the ballet *Hippolytus*

1902
Gouache and watercolour on paper, 28.7 x 40.8 cm
Russian Museum, St Petersburg

He showed no particular leaning to any of the essential core subjects: history, religion and life studies did not interest him, and it showed. He failed to shine in any field, and finally overstepped the limits of his teachers' patience when he produced an altogether too realistic representation of a religious subject. *The Lamentation of Christ* portrayed Mary as an old woman, red-eyed with weeping, and other characters exhibited pronounced Jewish features.

Design for the costume of a lady's maid at the court of Phaedra in the ballet *Hippolytus*

1902
29 x 21 cm
Private collection

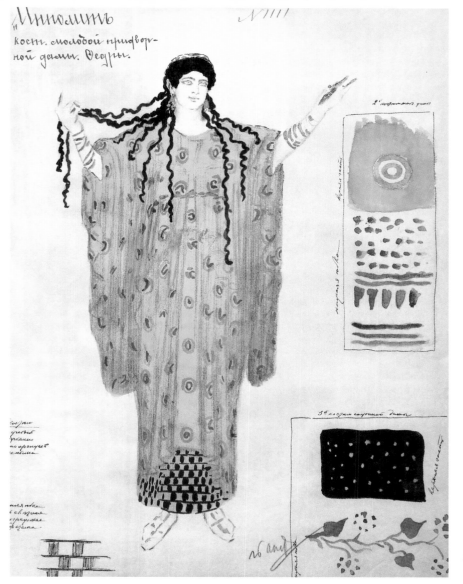

It was too much for the strait-laced, deeply conventional and probably racially-biased Academy of the 1880s.

By this time, his family's circumstances had altered for the worse following the recent death of his father. Bakst was forced to start looking for a means of providing financial support for himself and his mother and sisters.

After some searching, he was taken on as an illustrator at a studio that produced educational and children's books.

The Supper
───────────

1902
Oil on canvas, 150 x 100 cm
Russian Museum, St Petersburg

The owner of this educational enterprise, the writer Alexander Kanayev, took the young man under his wing and introduced him to various leading lights on the cultural scene, most notably Chekhov. Bakst came to know other artists as well as writers and publishers, and following his first commission from Kanayev found he was soon able to earn a modest living. Little of the work he produced during this early period was of any lasting value.

Design for the costume of the postman in the ballet *The Fairy Doll*

1903
Watercolour, bronze and Indian ink on paper, 37 x 20.3 cm
Russian Museum, St Petersburg

From 1888, however, when he illustrated editions of Shakespeare's *King Lear* and Schiller's *The Maid of Orléans* – rather dry drawings, dashed off without much effort or attention to detail – his style of book illustration gradually evolved, and he began to grasp the right balance between pictures and text. Making their first appearance were certain carnival themes, harlequins and masked dancers, that were to become almost motifs of the *Mir Iskusstva* circle.

Design for the costume of the French doll in the ballet *The Fairy Doll*

1903

His attraction to the otherworld of sorcery surfaced in depictions of demons and necromancers; his first tentative efforts at a black-and-white form of tachisme also appeared around this time. His pen and brush drawings for children's and young people's books began to earn him something of a name, and led to invitations to illustrate two books by A.V. Kruglov, *Happiness* and *Scenes from Russian Life*. A collaboration with the writer O.I. Rogova awoke in him a new interest in the life and cultures of different peoples.

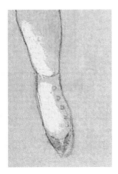

Design for the costume of the porcelain doll in the ballet *The Fairy Doll*

1903

But it was in his illustrations for newspaper and magazine articles, in *The Artist* and *St Petersburg Life*, that we see a clear indication of the main direction his work was later to take. Many of these illustrations were on theatrical themes, and two of them were completed at the joint première in 1892 of Tchaikovsky's opera *Iolanta* and his ballet *The Nutcracker*. Bakst's two great passions, drawing and the theatre, were coming together in a synthesis that would soon prove exciting.

Portrait of Lubov Gritsenko

1903
The State Tretyakov Gallery, Moscow

Russia and France
The Creation of the World of Art
1890-1909

For some time Bakst had been friendly with the well-known watercolour painter Albert Benois and his wife Marina, the daughter of a colleague on one of the journals he worked for. In the spring of 1890, when he was twenty-four, he met the artist's brother Alexander, then aged twenty. At first Benois and his friends felt sorry for the newcomer,

Portrait of Sergei Diaghilev and his Nurse
***
1904-1906
Oil on canvas, 97 x 83 cm
Russian Museum, St Petersburg

who told them how difficult he was finding it to make ends meet since his father had died. Pity soon turned to fondness, and the two very quickly became firm friends.

The group of friends took a keen interest in all matters cultural. They were up to date with the latest developments on the musical scene. They interminably discussed new literature. They were in close touch with the life of the theatre, particularly enjoying the frisson of going backstage at the Mariinsky, meeting the dancers and singers,

Portrait of Andrej Bely

1905

exchanging greetings with the wardrobe assistants, lighting technicians and props manager. All this was meat and drink to Bakst, whose own tastes had always been culturally inclined, and he was quickly taken into the bosom of this wonderfully lively circle.

Its moving spirits were, at first, Benois and the painter Konstantin Somov (1869-1939). The other members, both of whom had been at school with Somov and Benois, were Valery Nuvel, whose passion was music,

Vase (Self-Portrait)
_____

1906
Watercolour and gouache on paper mounted on canvas
113 x 71.3 cm
Russian Museum, St Petersburg

and Dimitri Filosofov, a philosopher and theologian who remained outside the main artistic thrust of the group and later the magazine. Diaghilev, who was Filosofov's cousin, was drawn into the group a few months later, in the summer, when Filosofov asked his friends to keep an eye on him while he was in St Petersburg to matriculate at the university. Once again, a warm friendship was almost immediately established.

Self-Portrait

1906

43

Brought up in Perm, a distant city within sight of the Ural Mountains, Diaghilev was part of a cultivated, musical family, and arranged to study singing, music theory and composition in the capital.

Bakst was invigorated and refreshed by his involvement with Benois and the group. Recognising that he needed to study further, he went to work with a will to remedy the deficiencies in his artistic education.

Portrait of Constantin Somov

1906
Charcoal, chalk on paper and cardboard, 35.5 x 26.7 cm
The State Tretyakov Gallery, Moscow

At first he examined the work of the great painters in the vast collections on view in the Hermitage, above all Rembrandt's portraits, which he attempted to copy. A year or so later, in June 1891, he decided to make an extended visit to western Europe. His first call was Paris, where he spent a great deal of time in the Luxembourg Museum. Next he went to Spain where, rather than copying the old masters, he preferred to paint landscape and scenes from nature.

Elysium

———

1906
The State Tretyakov Gallery, Moscow

He moved on to Italy, but found himself so enraptured by its beauties that he hardly allowed himself time to work. Returning to St Petersburg in September, he resumed working, rather half-heartedly, for newspapers and magazines in order to earn his living, but turned his real energies to studying watercolour under Benois' brother Albert, who was now president of the Society of Russian Watercolour Painters.

Terror Antiquus

1906
Decorative panel, oil on canvas, 250 x 270 cm
Russian Museum, St Petersburg

It was probably in this period that he decided to adopt a new name, based on his maternal grandmother's surname Bakster. He showed several works at the Society's regular exhibitions – nine in 1892, twelve the following year – from which it was clear that he had made enormous strides in his grasp of the medium. His highly developed sense of colour and attention to detail soon brought his work to the notice of the Grand Duke Vladimir, whose children he was invited to teach through the good offices of Benkendorf.

Downpour

1906
Gouache and indian ink on paper, 15.9 x 13.3 cm
Russian Museum, St Petersburg

His connection with the Imperial family, with whom he got on well, led to a commission for a large oil painting to mark the visit of a Russian naval detachment to France, and he left for Paris once more in 1893. The resultant painting, *Paris Welcoming Admiral Avelan*, was however not completed until 1900. This commission was not the sole reason for his departure to France. The rather naïve and inexperienced Bakst had fallen heavily for an actress some years older than himself, to the dismay of his mother and Benkendorf.

Portrait of the Poetess Zinaida Hippius

1906
Pencil and red and white chalk on paper mounted on cardboard, 54 x 44 cm
The State Tretyakov Gallery, Moscow

The two left for France together, staying at first in Brittany, and the trip turned into a protracted sojourn.

Although the passionate love affair came to an end after some three years, Bakst stayed for another three, punctuated by visits home, to Spain, where he was enraptured by Velázquez, and to North Africa, and it was during this entire period that he matured as an artist. He studied intently, attending the Académie Julian, where he was taught by Jean-Léon Gérôme, and learning much from the Finnish painter Albert Edelfelt.

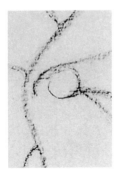

Portrait of Mili Balakirew

1907

L BAKST

He was fascinated by racial characteristics, and painted numerous watercolour portraits of different ethnic types. He strove to achieve a distinctive style, but it was a struggle he felt he succeeded in winning only in the fields of portraiture and landscape. He made portraits of Nuvel and Filosofov (1897). Longing to experiment, Bakst was held back by the harsh realities of the Parisian art market; but he did make progress in oil-painting, his brushwork becoming freer and more expressive.

In the Artist's Studio

Design for the poster of the Russian Painters' exhibition at the Vienna Secession
1908
Watercolour, gouache and black lead on paper mounted on cardboard, 46.8 x 60.2 cm

BAKST

Work continued on his huge commission, in which he depicted the arrival of the Admiral in the Place de la République amid a vast crowd. Friends came to visit him: Benois and his nephew Yevgeny Lanceray (1875-1946), and Diaghilev. These contacts reinforced the growing desire of the whole group to form a new artistic brotherhood that would provide a focus for the young talent bursting forth in Russia.

Design for the costume of Salomé in the ballet *Salomé*

1908
The State Tretyakov Gallery, Moscow

The name they decided on for their journal, *Mir Iskusstva* – The World of Art – attached itself also to the group, which thus became, almost officially, an artistic movement. The journal, founded in 1898, was to flourish spectacularly and its artists were to have a tremendous reforming impact on the whole concept of stage design, not just in Russia but throughout the world. It featured articles on music, art, theatre, literature and philosophy.

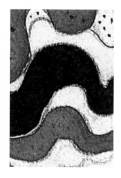

Ida Rubinstein as Salomé in the ballet *Salomé*

1908
45.5 x 29.5 cm

BAKST

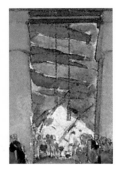

Everyone of any importance in the world of the arts either wrote for it or was the subject of an article in it. The artists whose work appeared in its pages tended either, like Benois and Somov, to follow Diaghilev's lead and return to the style of the eighteenth-century and Romantic painting, or to recreate the spirit of pagan Russia. All had a common goal: to absorb the manifold new currents emerging from the West and blend them with the most appealing traditional elements of Russian folk art.

Set design for the ballet *Cléopâtre*

1909

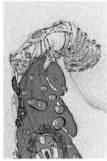

The renewal of this sense of tradition was one of the group's greatest strengths. It was the guiding impulse behind the wonderful range of artistic achievements that made their names reverberate around Europe during the first years of the new century. In the design of stage sets and costumes for the lyric arts – ballet and opera – there was no one else in Russia to touch them. In the graphic arts, too, they were unsurpassed: book and magazine illustration of the highest quality emerged from their studios.

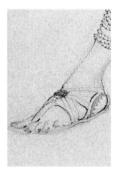

Design for the costume of Cleopatra for Ida Rubinstein in the ballet *Cléopâtre*

1909
28 x 21 cm
Mr. and Mrs. Lovanov-Rostovsky's Collection
The Metropolitan Museum of Art, New York

The role of Bakst in all this ferment of artistic activity was a prominent one. A vast range of opportunities opened up for him, and he was able to bring a new finish and focus to his work. And at last he was to find the perfect outlet for his creative talents: theatrical décor and costumes. Diaghilev's involvement with the theatre began when a close friend of his, Prince Sergei Volkonsky, was appointed Director of the Imperial Theatres in 1899 and took him on as his assistant.

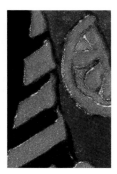

Design for the costume of a Jewish dancer in the ballet *Cléopâtre*

─────────────

1909 (dated 1910)
Watercolour, gouache, gold paint and pencil on paper
31.5 x 23 cm
Sotheby's, Private collection

Jobs were soon found for all the members of the circle. Bakst's first commission was to design a production of the French dance spectacle *The Marquise's Heart*, staged by the choreographer Marius Petipa in 1902.

In the meantime, Bakst could not afford to turn down work offered him by the new Director, Teliakovsky, in the face of Diaghilev's great indignation. To the artist's dismay, accusations of disloyalty were levelled at him.

Design for the costume of a satyr in the ballet *Cléopâtre*

1909 (dated 1910)
28 x 21.5 cm
Sotheby's, Private collection

CLÉOPATRE
„SATYRES"

BAKST
1910

He produced designs for two Greek tragedies, Euripides' *Hippolytus* (1902) and Sophocles' *Oedipus at Colonus* (1904) at the Alexandrinsky Theatre. Here he seized the chance to reincarnate the spirit of ancient Greece in a way that had never been done before, using the costumes to bring to life the characters of an immeasurably distant past. Bakst's sketches were so detailed and clear that the wardrobe staff found their task a simple one.

Design for the costume of an Indo-Persian dancer in the ballet *Cléopâtre*

1909
Watercolour and gold paint on paper, 48 x 31 cm
Private collection, Paris

71

For his designs the artist liked to sink into his characters, to eat, sleep and breathe their world, and he also liked to incorporate elements of each actor's or dancer's own personality – which the wearer understood and appreciated. Above all he strove for originality, an aim he triumphantly achieved.

At this time he was working on the ballet *The Fairy Doll*. This was staged by the Legat brothers, Nikolai and Sergei, in 1903 at the Hermitage Theatre, later moving to the much grander Mariinsky.

Design for the costume of Tamara Karsavina in the title-role of the ballet *The Firebird*

1910
35.5 x 26 cm
Sotherby's, Private collection

BAKST

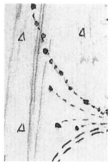

It was set in a toyshop, and Benois recounts that the source of Bakst's designs was the toyshop arcade in St Petersburg, which drew every child in the city like a magnet. The ballet and its sets and costumes were received with delight. Bakst achieved an ingenious contrast between the real and the fairy worlds, enlarging the scenic elements and props for the second act so that the dancers who played the dolls come to life looked tiny by comparison. This production marked the beginning of Bakst's true fame as a theatre designer.

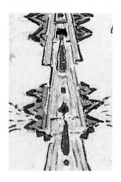

Design for the costume of Vera Fokina as Tsareva in the ballet *The Firebird*

1910
35.5 x 22.1 cm
State Museum of Theater and Music, St Petersburg

Bakst had by now met and fallen in love with Lubov Gritsenko, the widowed daughter of the famous art collector Prince P.M. Tretyakov. His love was expressed, curiously and somewhat comically, in the ballet's set, by giving Lubov's features and clothes to one of the dolls hanging from the toyshop ceiling. His friends found this hilariously funny, but Lubov must have been touched by the gesture since the couple were married not long afterwards.

Costume for the Firebird in the ballet *The Firebird*

1910
Watercolour and gouache on paper
Private collection

BAKST
1910

oiseau de feu

The marriage, in November 1903, did not take place without opposition from her family. To pacify them, Bakst agreed to convert from Judaism to Christianity – a decision that had consequences which were to affect the rest of his life. Bakst's and Lubov's only child, Andrei, was born in 1907. Lubov had a daughter, Marina, from her first marriage, of whom Bakst painted a charming portrait. Andrei's portrait of 1908 shows an enchanting, chubby little boy.

Costume for the Firebird in the ballet *The Firebird*

1910
Watercolour and gouache on paper
Private collection

Bakst produced paintings and watercolours in a variety of genres: portraits, narrative pieces and decorative panels. He also designed interiors, notably that of Alexander Korovin's house in St Petersburg. Bakst's other great strength, his graphic work, was being perfected during this period. Like the Impressionists and the Decadents in France, he was drawn to Japanese prints, now circulating outside their country of origin for the first time, and started collecting them, particularly those of Hokusai.

Set design for the harem in the ballet *Shéhérazade*

1910
Watercolour on paper
Musée des Arts Décoratifs, Paris

He loved their bright, fresh colours, their economy of line and their often unexpected viewpoint. His contributions to the new *Mir Iskusstva* journal were completely different in character from his earlier work for children's books and newspapers: now he designed the whole page as a complete entity. Another innovation: he and Somov created a radical new look for theatre programmes, making them for the first time colourful, beautiful objects in their own right that a theatre-goer would want to keep as a souvenir.

Design for the costume of Alexis Boulgakov as Shâh Shâhriyâr in the ballet *Shéhérazade*

1910
35.5 x 22 cm
Thyssen-Bornemisza Collection, Madrid

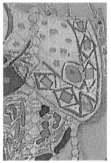

At about this time, anxious to propagate the innovative approach of the World of Art and its adherents, and noting with dismay that the stagnation of academicism was still weighing heavily on art studies, he was invited to teach, along with Mstislav Dobuzhinsky, at Yelizaveta Zvantseva's liberal school of painting – one of whose later students was Marc Chagall.

Although the journal had ceased publication by 1904, the World of Art exhibitions continued.

Design for the costume of a Great Eunuch in the ballet *Shéhérazade*

1910
Musée des Beaux-Arts, Strasbourg

Within two years the group had taken under their umbrella a large number of artists who were not closely connected with the original six. The broad range of styles and the eclectic aesthetic approach of these new members contributed to the richness and diversity of the movement that was to make such a mark in the history of Russian art. The group now included Mikhail Vrubel, Bilibin, Roerich, Igor Grabar, Valentin Serov, Dobuzhinsky, Alexander Golovin, Yevgeny Lanceray and Anna Ostroumova-Lebedeva.

Design for the costume of a Great Eunuch in the ballet *Shéhérazade*

1910
National Gallery of Australia, Canberra

In 1910, following a quarrel with the Union of Russian Artists in Moscow, with whom they were affiliated, the group would secede and form the "official" World of Art movement. The Imperial Ballet Company at the Mariinsky Theatre still had the highest technical standards and, indeed, was the training-ground for the talents of the great dancers, whose names we now utter with reverence. But by now many of the grand ballets were formulaic: little innovation had been allowed for the last hundred years.

Design for the costume of the Silber Niger in the ballet *Shéhérazade*

1910

Occasionally, charity performances were given at the Mariinsky, for which choreographers were allowed greater freedom. It was at one such evening in 1907 that Anna Pavlova, already a dazzling star, first performed the number that was to become her signature piece, *The Dying Swan*. The music – not in fact intended by the composer to depict the swan's demise – was from Saint-Saëns' *Carnival of the Animals*, and the eloquent choreography perfectly encapsulated Pavlova's infinite expressiveness. The exquisite swan costume was designed by Bakst.

Design for the costume of the Gold Niger in the ballet *Shéhérazade*

1910
35.5 x 22 cm
Musée des Beaux-Arts, Strasbourg

5 NEGRES

L BAKST
1910

91

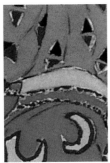

Enmeshed as he was in theatre design, Bakst was nonetheless continuing to paint for the World of Art exhibitions. In 1907, he fulfilled a long-held ambition when he went on an extended visit to the classical sites of Greece in the company of Valentin Serov. On his return he did some notable landscapes, but one of his most impressive paintings was the decorative panel *Terror Antiquus*, the subject of which was the destruction of the legendary city of Atlantis.

Design for the costume of an Odalisque based on the ballet *Shéhérazade*

1911
The Marion Koogler McNay Art Museum, San Antonio

BAKST
1910

The tiny figures rushing about show the puniness of mankind when confronted with the wayward will of the gods. The swirling waters contrast with the "archaic smile" of Aphrodite in the foreground, clearly copied from the *kore* figures that he must have seen on his Greek trip. The panel went on to win the first Gold Medal of the Brussels International Exhibition in 1910.

Drawing of Vaslav Nijinsky in the ballet *Shéhérazade*

1911

Encouraged by the warmth of the reception in Europe for all things Russian and filled with confidence in the radical reforms being introduced by Fokine, Diaghilev formulated his next venture. The Ballets Russes was born from a number of conversations between all the eventual participants, each of whom believed he or she had persuaded Diaghilev to try out the idea. In fact, the wily impresario had been thinking along such lines for some time.

Design for the costume of the Blue Sultana in the ballet *Shéhérazade*

1910
Watercolour, gouache and gold paint on paper
Private collection

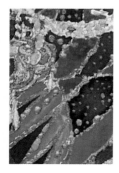

Bakst, Benois and Nuvel were brought in to plan the new Paris season for 1909. Fokine was to create a new ballet: *Cléopâtre*, which Bakst was commissioned to design. For this ballet Bakst carried out a conscientious study of Egyptian reliefs, and it was from his sketches that Fokine devised characteristic movement for his dancers: head turned in profile, arms and body facing forward.

The cast – a balletomane's dream – included Pavlova and Fokine, Karsavina and Nijinsky.

Design for the costume of Shâh Zaman in the ballet *Shéhérazade*

1910
National Gallery of Australia, Canberra

BAKST
1910

The dancer selected to play Cleopatra was a young unknown, Ida Rubinstein (1885-1960). An exotic creature, tall and very thin, with haunting dark eyes, she was not a professional dancer but had made a considerable impression on Fokine. She was quick to recognise Bakst's happy knack of incorporating something of the dancer's personality in his designs – he did the costumes for one of her earliest solo appearances, in a ballet based on another

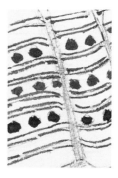

Design for the costume of Ludmilla Schollar as Estrell in the ballet *Carnaval*

1910
31.5 x 24.5 cm
State Museum of Theater and Music, St Petersburg

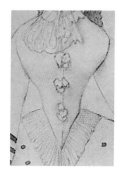

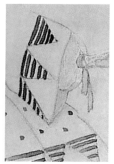

Greek tragedy, *Antigone*, and produced a dramatic design for her as Oscar Wilde's *Salome*, although that particular production was never staged. The two formed a close and lasting working relationship, which was to add lustre to her reputation in Europe.

Cléopâtre was a dance-drama, in which conventional ballet steps had little part. Bakst's extremely stylish set consisted of an Egyptian temple with ranks of pillars and vast statues. Bakst's spatial grasp and colour sense earned him a reception rarely accorded a designer.

Design for the costume of the "valse noble" in the ballet *Carnaval*

1910

The other ballets given in this inaugural season were *Le Pavillon d'Armide* and *Les Sylphides*; operas were Rimsky-Korsakov's *Ivan the Terrible* and Serov's *Judith*.

The tour was a magnificent triumph for Diaghilev and for his company. The dancers were well on their way to becoming legends, but what was really new was the importance of the designer's role. Bakst, Benois and their colleagues made an unforgettable and permanent impact on theatre design.

Design for the costume of Chiarina in the ballet *Carnaval*

1910
Watercolour and pencil on paper, 27.5 x 21 cm
State Museum of Theater and Music, St Petersburg

КАРНАВАЛ ШУМАНА
Chiarina

BAKST
10

Towards a Coloured Universe
1910-1913

The period just before the outbreak of World War I saw an unparalleled outpouring of artistic riches from Diaghilev's Ballets Russes. With their first proper season behind them, all the artists associated with the company, whether dancers, choreographers, composers or painters, felt a surge of confidence which was translated into the most glorious results.

Costume for Chiarina in the ballet *Carnaval*

1910
National Gallery of Australia, Canberra

Almost every one of the ballets that now emerged was a masterpiece – a synthesis of music, dance, drama and design that still takes the breath away. The members of the World of Art had always been passionate about the theatre, and felt that the greatest compliment their works could receive was to be described as "theatrical". Music, too, had always been a passion. As well as their own heroes these artists knew the great composers outside Russia, and idolised Wagner as well as Tchaikovsky, Chopin as well as Glinka.

Design for the costume of Vaslav Nijinsky as Prince Iskender in the ballet *La Péri*

1911
Watercolour, 67.6 x 48.9 cm
The Metropolitan Museum of Art, New York

But living composers such as Claude Debussy, Richard Strauss, Maurice Ravel and Manuel de Falla were now coming to the fore and were about to play a large part in the next instalments of the Ballets Russes story. Above all, among the newer generation was the towering genius of the young Igor Stravinsky.

Bakst rode high on the crest of this creative wave. Indeed, between 1909 and 1921 he designed more productions for Diaghilev than anyone else, even Benois.

Design for the costume of Natasha Trouhanova in the title-role of the ballet *La Péri*

1911
Watercolour and gouache on paper, 68 x 48.5 cm
Lobanova-Rostovsky Collection
The Metropolitan Museum of Art, New York

His designs for many of the ballets of this period remain imprinted on the memory. He reached his zenith as an artist of the theatre, and it is no exaggeration to say that the words Ballets Russes conjure up for many people the swirling, fluttering shapes, the sumptuous fabrics and the intense, vividly contrasting colours of Bakst's inspiration.

After the astonishing impact of that first 1909 season, everyone needed to rest and to recharge the batteries with fresh ideas.

Design for the costume of Nijinsky as Narcissus in the ballet *Narcisse*

1911
State Museum of Theater and Music, St Petersburg

P. "NARCISSE"
(Nijinsky)

Diaghilev, who by this time was in love with Nijinsky and had almost certainly begun a physical affair with him, took the young star on an extended trip to Venice, his favourite city. Bakst went with them, possibly as something of a chaperone. In Venice Bakst made a big oil sketch of Nijinsky on the beach, his tanned, muscular physique contrasting with the blue of the sea and the bright red of his bathing trunks.

Design for the costume of a Beotian Woman in the ballet *Narcisse*

1911
40 x 27.3 cm
State Museum of Theater and Music, St Petersburg

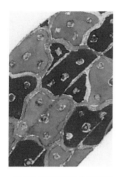

Nijinsky (1888-1950) was to create memorable roles in the ballets that made Diaghilev's name: the Golden Slave in *Shéhérazade* and the title roles in *Petrushka* and *Le Spectre de la rose*. More than that, he was to choreograph and dance in two of the most mould-breaking ballets to come out of the Diaghilev crucible: *L'Après-Midi d'un faune* (A Faun's Afternoon) *and Le Sacre du Printemps* (The Rite of Spring). But this meteor of the balletic firmament soon burnt out.

Design for the costume of a Beotian Man in the ballet *Narcisse*

———————————

1911
40 x 27.3 cm
State Museum of Theater and Music, St Petersburg

NARCISSE

His marriage to a dancer in the company, Romola de Pulszky, in 1913 caused an immediate, bitter split with Diaghilev, and he declined into schizophrenia only a few years later, at the age of thirty-one.

In Venice, Bakst drank in the beauties of the churches and palaces, was absorbed by the paintings of Titian and Tintoretto, and was seduced by the charm of the picturesque gondolas, the bridges and canals. The whole experience made a deep impression on him.

Designs for the costumes of two young Beotians, Vera Fokina and Bronislava Nijinska in the ballet *Narcisse*

1911
Watercolour, gouache, pencil and gold paint on paper
47 x 32 cm
Private collection

NARCISSE BÉOTNIENES

119

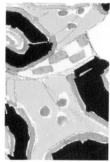

His style underwent a radical change, and in June the Russian newspapers carried the story that he had sent for all his old canvases and burned them. The impetus behind this unnecessarily dramatic gesture was not just the glories of the Venetian Renaissance. Bakst was by now familiar with the saturated colours and bold forms of the French Post-Impressionists, in particular Gauguin and Matisse, and their uncompromising modernism made him see his own style in a new light.

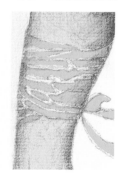

Design for the costume of a young shepherd in the ballet *Narcisse*

1911
Watercolour, pencil and gold paint on paper
Private collection

NARCISSE
BRUSHIAN

121

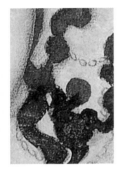

The change was not a sudden one – it had been growing in him for some time – but it was the catalyst of his Venice visit that released his full artistic creativity. Somehow Diaghilev, the eternal optimist, managed to pull a financial rabbit out of the hat, with the aid of the long-suffering Astruc, and the Ballets Russes company was reassembled in Paris for the 1910 season. Exciting ideas for the programme slowly began to take shape.

Design for the costume of a nymph in the ballet *Narcisse*

1911
40 x 26.8 cm
Musée des Beaux-Arts, Strasbourg

Everyone agreed that a new ballet on a Russian theme was highly desirable. Heads were put together and eventually came up with the folktale of *The Firebird,* considerably adapted from the published version. Benois wanted to mount a production of the seventy-year-old French ballet *Giselle* as a graceful compliment to the original home of the art. He was also responsible for initiating the concept of *Shéhérazade.*

Design for the costume of the First Bacchante in the ballet *Narcisse*

1911
State Museum of Theater and Music, St Petersburg

Fokine had been inspired to create *Le Carnaval* by a request for an entertainment at a ball in St Petersburg, and Diaghilev was persuaded to take it over.

There was anxiety before the opening of the season – no opera this year, no Pavlova (she had by now decided to start her own company, finding herself out of sympathy with Fokine's innovative style and Stravinsky's strange new music, and, less nobly, motivated by jealousy of Karsavina).

Design for the costume of a bacchante
in the ballet *Narcisse*

1911
Frontispiece for the Official Program of the Russian Ballets
31 x 20 cm
Sotheby's, Private collection

PROGRAMME OFFICIEL
DES
BALLETS RUSSES

Costume de "NARCISSE"

But the new ballets were destined to be rapturously received. *Shéhérazade*, in particular, was a sure-fire gilt-edged success. The music was the lushly melodic symphonic poem by Rimsky-Korsakov, who had worked out a programme for it based loosely on the tales from the *1001 Arabian Nights*. Benois, however, thought up a completely different story-line: the sultan Shâhriyâr and his brother Zaman plan to test the faithfulness of his wives, above all his favourite, Zobeida.

Set design for Act I of the ballet *The Martyrdom of St Sebastian*

1911
42 x 57.3 cm
Sotheby's, Private collection

They pretend to go off hunting but return to find an orgy in full swing: Zobeida and her lover, the Golden Slave, are caught *in flagrante*. The Sultan, heartbroken, orders the killing of all the wives and the Negro slaves – Zobeida alone is spared, but when he catches sight of the body of her lover, he stabs her.

Bakst designed the production, and made many suggestions on how the story-line should run. Benois was dismayed to find that in the programme Bakst was credited as the author.

Poster showing the designs for costumes of secondary characters in the ballet *The Martyrdom of St Sebastian*

1911
13 x 40 cm
Sotheby's, Private collection

E MARTYRE DE SAINT SEBASTIEN

This caused a major row between him and Diaghilev, although he seems not to have harboured bitter feelings towards Bakst. The role of Zobeida was danced by Ida Rubinstein; Nijinsky was of course the Golden Slave. Both these extraordinary individuals, in Fokine's dramatic choreography, made a terrific impact. But the biggest sensation of all was created by Bakst's designs. Before getting down to work he had undertaken an intensive study of the art of the Persian miniature as well as Turkish and Chinese art. The fruit of this study was a décor of unparalleled luxury.

Design for a costume in the ballet *The Martyrdom of St Sebastian*

1911

« Il faut que chacun
tue son amour pour qu'il revive
sept fois plus ardent. »

Gabriele d'Annunzio

BAKST

ST·SEBASTIEN
(Mme JDA RUBINSTEIN)

The costumes were, if anything, an even greater triumph. The designer's Oriental studies had fired his imagination to create clothes of an almost outrageous sensuality. The blue and crimson outfit for the sultan Shâhriyâr – a mime role, taken by the outstanding mime artist Alexander Bulgakov – and his brother Zaman are superb; sultan Shâhriyâr's is obviously too cumbersome to be danced in, although his brother's is less restrictive.

Design for the accessories and furnishings
in the ballet *Le Spectre de la rose*

1911
39 x 26 cm
Sotheby's, Private collection

table de Toilette avec objets de toilette
1 banquette

1 Table ronde avec vase en verre
et quantité de violettes

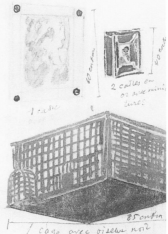

1 cadre

2 cadres en
or avec minia-
tures

40 cent.

85 cent.

1 cage avec oiseau noir
dedans, la cage s'attache
au plafond devant la fe-
nêtre du gauche (du public)

1 divant avec 3 coussins

Bakst.

135

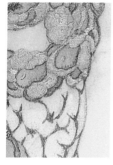

The Chief Eunuch's outfit of brilliant scarlet is sumptuous, a fitting tribute to the great dancer and teacher Enrico Cecchetti who took the role. The odalisques, their pinks and greens echoing the silk curtain, and the dancing girls in their transparent veiling were costumed like a voluptuary's dream. Zobeida herself was decked in pearls and tassels; her role, written for Rubinstein, was not a virtuoso one and presumably she did not have too much vigorous jumping and pirouetting to contend with.

Design for the costume of Vaslav Nijinsky in the ballet *Le Spectre de la rose*

1911
40 x 28.5 cm
Ella Gallup Sumner and Mary Catlin Sumner Collection
Wadsworth Atheneum, Hartford

SPECTRE DE LA ROSE

NIJINSKY

BAKST
1911

137

The most extraordinary costumes of all were reserved for the Negro slaves. A kind of gilded bustier was attached to the voluminous trousers and to the neckpiece with strings of pearls, while the head was bound turban fashion with a scarf on which beads on "trembler" springs were mounted. Nijinsky's androgynous beauty and sinuous line were emphasised to the full by the glamour of his costume. These trembler springs were one of a number of elements that would influence jewellery

Set design for the prelude to the ballet
L'Après-Midi d'un faune

1912
75 x 105 cm
Musée national d'art moderne, Centre Georges Pompidou
Paris

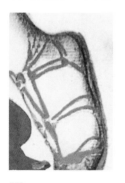

design and fashion for some years to come. Cartier, the great jewellery firm, took up the blue and green theme in some magnificent necklaces and other pieces. Orientalism became all the rage in furnishings and interiors. The Paris couturier Paul Poiret adopted an Oriental theme in his collections both before and after the Great War; a houseboat interior he designed for the 1925 World's Fair is filled with huge soft cushions. Turbans were everywhere.

Design for the costume of Nijinsky in the ballet
L'Après-Midi d'un faune

1912
Watercolour, gouache and gold paint on paper mounted on cardboard, 40 x 27 cm
Musée d'Orsay, Paris

Every society hostess, every leader of fashion, such as the extraordinary Marchesa Casati, wanted a salon like the interior of Bakst's harem. The influence spread to architecture, and even, a little later, to the newborn art of film. The rich arabesques of *Shéhérazade* were reflected in Rudolph Valentino's *The Sheikh* of 1921. If ever there was a moment when the world lay at Bakst's feet, this was it.

Costume for a nymph in the ballet
L'Après-Midi d'un faune

1912

Bakst was endowed with a singular gift in designing his costumes. Somehow the actual fabric, and the way it was cut and draped, had the subtle effect of encouraging the dancer's movements to fit the setting or period depicted in the ballet. In the same way, he could use colour to express feeling and dramatic tension, reinforcing the emotions produced by the music and the choreography in an almost uncanny way.

Costume for a nymph in the ballet
L'Après-Midi d'un faune

1912

This way of interpreting the music through colour was something completely new in ballet. One critic commented that the Russians were able to create an astonishing harmony between music and décor, which gave the impression of sound arising from colour and colour from music. The second great sensation of the 1910 season was *L'Oiseau de Feu* (The Firebird). Bakst was not so deeply involved with the designs for this ballet, but he was of course keenly interested

Costumes for nymphs in the ballet
L'Après-Midi d'un faune

1912
National Gallery of Australia, Canberra

in so unprecedented a project, and found himself designing the costumes for the principal roles, that of the Firebird herself, the Tsarevich and the Beautiful Tsarevna. The Firebird's yellow, red and orange costume, sparkling with gold ornament, was a dramatic contrast to the gentle Tsarevna's flowing white gown with its relatively restrained decoration of stylised geometrical figures and roses.

Set design for the Act I of the ballet *Helen of Sparta*

1912
Oil on canvas, 132 x 187 cm

What really broke the mould and launched the art of ballet into the twentieth century was Stravinsky's music. Although he was a pupil of Rimsky-Korsakov and there are resonances of his master, nothing quite like this had been heard before. The discordant exuberance of the *Dance of the Infernal Spirits* still affects the listener just as it must have done in 1910 – a blast from the winds of hell on to the sophisticated audience at the Paris Opéra.

Set design for the Act II of the ballet *Helen of Sparta*

1912
Oil on paper, 55.5 x 57 cm
Galleria del Levante, Milan

A entertainment called *Le Festin* (The Festival), a group of show-stopping numbers from various ballets, was put together to make up a full repertoire. One of Bakst's designs for this was an incarnation of Nijinsky as the Hindu Prince, a costume strongly influenced by the Persian miniatures he had studied for *Shéhérazade*. He also made a costume for Karsavina as the Golden Bird. These two were fairytale characters in the *pas de deux (in fact the "Blue Bird")* from the last act of *The Sleeping Princess*.

Design for the costume of Desjardins as Menelaus in the ballet *Helen of Sparta*

1912
26 x 24 cm
Parmenia Migel Ekstrom Collection, New York

Yet another triumphant première of the 1910 season was *Le Carnaval*, choreographed by Fokine to Schumann's piano suite of 1834. Bakst's designs for this ballet were in radical contrast to those he had come up with for the Oriental work. He adopted the rather saccharine style typical of the period when the work was composed, while not losing sight of the characters' *Commedia dell' Arte* origins.

Bakst, along with his colleague Nikolai Roerich, was very much drawn to the art of Gauguin and Matisse.

Design for the costume of Ida Rubinstein as Helen in Act IV of the ballet *Helen of Sparta*

1912
Bibliothèque nationale de France, Musée de l'Opéra, Paris

155

Gauguin's colours came, he thought, somewhere between medieval stained-glass windows and the dazzling palette of Veronese, while his perception of form also had its effect on the Russian painter. Matisse too was a hero, and the two met for the first time in that summer of 1910, to Bakst's joy. After a success such as they had had in 1910, there was no doubt in anyone's mind that the Ballets Russes would reassemble the following year.

Set design for the ballet *Salomé*

1912
45.9 x 62.5 cm
Ashmolean Museum, Oxford

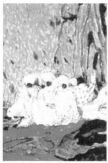

Through a combination of happy circumstances, Diaghilev was able to form it into a permanent company, with Karsavina and Nijinsky as full-time stars. Bakst was now part of the Parisian artistic establishment. In 1911, he was elected a vice-president of the jury panel of the des Arts Décoratifs, and had his first one-man show – an exhibition of 120 stage designs – at the society's museum.

Set design for the ballet *Le Dieu bleu*

1911
Chalk, watercolour and gouache on paper
55.8 x 78 cm
Musée national d'art moderne, Centre Georges Pompidou
Paris

That year Diaghilev made him artistic director of the company.

Bakst's loyalty to Diaghilev and the company was never in doubt, but he felt he could not put all his eggs in one basket; besides, he was very close to both Anna Pavlova and Ida Rubinstein, neither of whom felt under similar moral obligations. His friendship with Rubinstein was a fruitful one. When she came up with a daring new project, it was to Bakst that she turned in order to be costumed in suitably mesmerising style.

Design for the costume of Bayadère in the ballet *Le Dieu bleu*

1912
Watercolour, pencil and gold on paper, 58.2 x 43 cm
Private collection

3 BAIADERES AVEC PAON
DIEU BLEU

BAKST
1911

161

The project was an ambitious one: *Le Martyre de saint Sébastien* (The Martyrdom of St Sebastian), a "stage spectacle" rather than a ballet, conceived by the Italian novelist and poet Gabriele D'Annunzio (1863-1938), with music by Claude Debussy. D'Annunzio thought Rubinstein "a sibyl listening to the god within her". After seeing her in *Cléopâtre* he declared that her legs were those of St Sebastian, for which he had been vainly searching for years.

Design for the costume of a temple dancer in the ballet *Le Dieu bleu*

1912
Watercolour, pencil and gold on paper, 43 x 28 cm
Musée national d'art moderne, Centre Georges Pompidou
Paris

When they met – an encounter orchestrated by that past master of the Decadence, Count Robert de Montesquiou – they competed in exchanging extravagant compliments. Bakst's sets were said to have re-created the splendour of Byzantium, the mystique of the Gothic cathedral. But its elaborate staging and enormous length did not lead to the dizzy success that its author had anticipated. Yet again, although Rubinstein herself was ecstatically applauded for her embodiment of the martyred saint,

Design for the costume of the Blue God in the ballet *Le Dieu bleu*

1912

165

the spotlight fell on Bakst's designs, which were judged to be among his finest achievements.

This act of infidelity, as he saw it, on the part of Bakst and Rubinstein went down very badly with Diaghilev. Fokine, too, had joined the traitors, creating the dances for the spectacular show. Then Rubinstein let him down, by not turning up for her scheduled performances in *Shéhérazade*. Not only that: Diaghilev was negotiating with Debussy for a new work, and he was put out that the

Costume of the Blue God in the ballet *Le Dieu bleu*

1912
National Gallery of Australia, Canberra

composer had seized so enthusiastically on the D'Annunzio project. Diaghilev's bitterness erupted in a strongly-worded letter to Astruc: *"Bakst claims that we lack confidence in his work, but I must say that I have never seen so astounding a betrayal of every artistic and aesthetic principle as he has shown in his dealings with us."*

The programme for the new season was to take shape in Monte Carlo, where the company would open in April.

Design for the costume of a young rajah
in the ballet *Le Dieu bleu*

1912
Bibliothèque nationale de France, Musée de l'Opéra, Paris

"DIEU BLEU"
JEUNES RAJAS

BAKST
1911

169

Bakst was very busy in Paris with Ida and *St Sebastian*, and had to be forced by Diaghilev to come down to the Mediterranean and start work on one of the new ballets assigned to him. *Le Spectre de la rose*, a *pas de deux* for Nijinsky and Karsavina to Weber's *Invitation to the Dance*, orchestrated by Berlioz, had already been choreographed by Fokine in St Petersburg. Bakst chose the 1830s for his charming setting of a young girl's moonlit bedroom.

Design for the costume of a pilgrim
in the ballet *Le Dieu bleu*

1912
43 x 28 cm
Thyssen-Bornemisza Collection, Madrid

"DIEU BLEU"
PÈLERIN

BAKST
1911

The girl, newly returned from her first ball, was dressed in a flounced white gown. The spirit of the rose was clad entirely, so it seemed, in petals of various shades of pink, red and mauve, while the headdress was made up of rose leaves. The designer demonstrated yet again his ability to match the costume perfectly to the music and the choreography.

As always, the designs played a large part in the production's success.

Design for the costume of the bride
in the ballet *Le Dieu bleu*

1912

„DIEU BLEU"
„LA FIANCÉE"

BAKST
1911

173

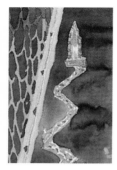

The most splendid triumphs were still to come, when the company moved on to Paris. *Petrushka* was the highlight of the season, a peerless combination of the designs of Benois, the choreography of Fokine, the performance of Nijinsky as the pathetic clown puppet with a human heart, and the wonderful music of Stravinsky, evoking so convincingly the Shrovetide fair of old St Petersburg. Bakst had no hand in this, but he did produce designs for a ballet on the classical myth of Narcissus and Echo.

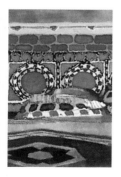

Set design for the ballet *Thamar*

1912
Musée des Arts Décoratifs, Paris

He was also scheduled to design two further works, *La Péri* and *Le Dieu bleu*. Eventually the rift was smoothed over, but relations between Bakst and Diaghilev were never quite to be as relaxed and close as they had once been. It was soon clear why the impresario could not do without his designer. The company's London season, timed to coincide with the coronation of King George V in June, unleashed an unprecedented fit of Bakstomania.

Queen Thamar and the Prince in the ballet *Thamar*

1912
Program cover, *Comœdia Illustré* (1912)

Comœdia Illustré

Mᵐᵉ KARSAVINA et Mʳ BOLM dans THAMAR.

Polychrome Comœdia Illustré   Costumes dessinés par Léon BAKST.

177

The windows of the fashionable shops and department stores were filled with brilliant colours and luxurious fabrics; the harem had become respectable. In spite of the row over *St Sebastian*, Bakst was not deterred from creating the sets and costumes for another Rubinstein vehicle. For *Helen of Sparta,* by Emile Verhaeren (1912), he did three sets, all expressing his very individual conception of the landscape of ancient Greece.

Costume for Queen Thamar in the ballet *Thamar*

1912
National Museum of Australia, Canberra

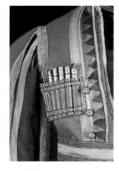

By the 1912 season, all was not entirely well with the Ballets Russes. The public, which had received them so enthusiastically for three seasons, was beginning to be a little critical, and the first failures could be discerned. *Narcisse* was one of them; another was *Daphnis and Chloë*, which, in spite of Ravel's ravishing music and Fokine's lyrical dances, did not find the success it deserved.

In Diaghilev the feeling grew that the blame for this less-than-perfect state of affairs lay, in part at least, with Fokine's

Costume for a Lezghin in the ballet *Thamar*

1912
National Museum of Australia, Canberra

choreography, which he and Stravinsky thought was running out of inspiration. He encouraged Nijinsky to experiment with his own choreographic efforts, the first fruit of which was *L'Après-Midi d'un faune*, but for the time being kept it a dark secret from everyone – he did not want Fokine to know. Work on *Thamar* and *Le Dieu bleu* meanwhile went ahead. On both of these, Fokine collaborated with Bakst for what was to be very nearly the last time.

Set design for Acts I and III of the ballet
Daphnis and Chloë

1912
Watercolour on paper, 74 x 103.5 cm
Musée des Arts Décoratifs, Paris

Le Dieu bleu was another Oriental piece, this time on a Hindu theme. The libretto was by Jean Cocteau, the music by Reynaldo Hahn; Nijinsky was of course to dance the title role . With the involvement of Fokine and Bakst this was, on the face of it, an unbeatable combination.

The other ballet, *Thamar*, recalled the triumph of *Shéhérazade* with its exotically colourful score by Balakirev, one of Rimsky-Korsakov's early circle.

Set design for the Act II of the ballet
Daphnis and Chloë

―――――――――――

1912
Musée des Arts Décoratifs, Paris

185

The story, adapted by Bakst from the poem by Lermontov, blends the erotic and the morbid. Thamar, Queen of Georgia, has her lovers put to death after they have served their purpose. Karsavina's partner as the doomed prince was Adolph Bolm, a fine dancer who specialised in character roles. The colours of the set ranged from pink to dark red and deep purple. The brick-walled octagonal tower rose menacingly to the flies, engendering an atmosphere of unease and mystery.

Design for the costume of Tamara Karsavina as Chloë in the ballet *Daphnis and Chloë*

1912
Wadsworth Atheneum Museum of Art, Hartford

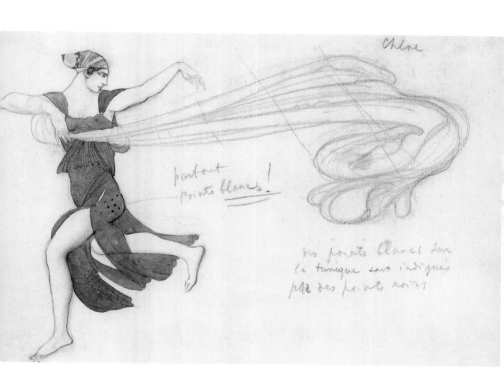

Chloé

partout
points blancs !

les points blancs sur
la tunique sont indiqués
plus des points noirs

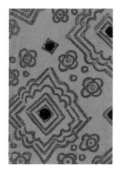

The glow of the setting sun, dappling the dark blue floor and the green carpet, streamed in via the tall windows, through which distant snowy mountains could be glimpsed. Again the ballet was not an immediate popular success, although it was critically acclaimed in some quarters. One critic thought that Bakst's production perfectly encapsulated the essence of the Caucasus.

Fokine, too, was unhappy. He had put his all into *Daphnis and Chloë*, wanting it to stand as one of his greatest achievements,

Design for the costume of a Polish officer

1913
26.3 x 21 cm
Parmenia Migel Ekstrom Collection, New York

Дорогому
Валериан Костичну
Светиону
на добрую память
от автора приношение
Лев Бакст
Paris
1913.

BORIS GODOUNOU
POLONAIS

Bakst

but he felt anxious at the state of the company. Standards were slipping because many of the most experienced dancers, worried about severing links with their homeland now that the company was a permanent one, had left to return to Russia. When he finally found out about *L'Après-Midi d'un faune*, it was to be told that its première was to come before that of *Daphnis*. Fokine's resentment and bitterness at the slight to his position boiled over.

Design for the set of the prologue of the ballet
The Pisanelle or *The Perfumed Death*

1913
Extract of *Comœdia Illustré* (20 June 1913)

There was an explosive meeting with Diaghilev, and he was compelled to leave the company he had done so much to shape.

L'Après-Midi d'un faune revealed a revolutionary approach that was to affect ballet throughout the twentieth century and confirm the dancer as a ballet-maker of a strange and rare genius. The short work, to music of startling sensuousness by Debussy, is simply the faun's erotic dreams brought to life. The movements echo those familiar from Greek friezes.

Set design for the ballet *Oriental Fantasy*

1913

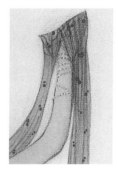

The seven nymphs – at the première they included Olga Kokhlova, later Picasso's first wife – were dressed in long pleated tunics in cream with a blue or brownish pattern. The faun – half-human half-creature – was clad in a kind of body-stocking with piebald markings, like the skin of an animal. Two little gold horns grew from his head; his make-up, including the pointed ears, exaggerated the animal quality of the dancer's actual features.

Design for the costume of Anna Pavlova in the ballet *Oriental Fantasy*

1913
Victoria & Albert Museum, London

BALLET HINDOU
MADAME A. PAVLOVA

BAKST
1913

195

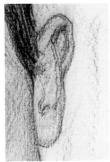

The choreography departed so radically from anything created before that Bakst realised he was witnessing the end of the old order. Even Fokine's most drastic reforms had never gone anything like as far as this. The ballet caused outrage as well as ecstatic applause – outrage because at the first performance Nijinsky lay down on the chief nymph's purloined veil and thrust himself at it in an unequivocal act of passion.

Portrait of Leonide Massine

1914

A grand scandal broke out, in which an influential newspaper editor, taking a high moral tone, and the defenders of artistic freedom, notably Rodin and Redon, attacked each other with gusto. The whole affair blew up out of all proportion into a wide-ranging assault on modernity in all its aspects. Tickets for the ballet sold like hot cakes. Nijinsky was dismayed, Diaghilev delighted. Bakst's personal life was not going well at this point either.

Design for the costume of young men leading Orpheu to the temple in Act I of the ballet *Orphée*

1914

ОРФЕЙ Tarts
Jeunes Jens con
disant ORPHEE
au TEMPLE.

BAKST
1914

He was tired, heavily overworked, and for some time had been suffering from what was clearly clinical depression. Despite his illness, Bakst soldiered on into 1913. Among the projects that he took on his shoulders was another Rubinstein spectacle, *La Pisanelle*, again by D'Annunzio. The costumes were inspired by the Renaissance painter Carpaccio, and the close collaboration of Bakst and Fokine – their last – made something splendid out of fairly mediocre material.

Design for the costume of a monster
in the ballet *Orphée*

1914
24.5 x 31 cm
The Pushkin Museum of Fine Arts, Moscow

"ORPHÉE"
"DACTE,AIDE"
"MONSTRES"

BAKST

In London, he did the settings for two operas: productions of Boito's *Mefistofele* and Wolf-Ferrari's *Il Segreto di Susanna* for Covent Garden. His first English one-man show took place at the Fine Art Society, which also published a monograph by Arsène Alexandre, *L'Art décoratif de Leon Bakst* ("The Decorative Art of Leon Bakst"). There was a visit to Germany to look at Nuremberg, Cologne and Dresden, in the expectation of doing a production of Gounod's *Faust*, which did not come off.

Design for Putiphar's Wife in the ballet
La Légende de Joseph

1914
Watercolour, pencil and gold paint on paper
Private collection

Dessin de Léon BAKST pour le costume de Mme KOUSNETZOFF (Rôle de la femme de Putiphar)

He designed several productions for Pavlova's company; he had remained on very good terms with her, and it was she who opened his first one-man show in New York, because he was unable to get there and she was touring the USA at the time. In the same year, 1913, Bakst's self-portrait shows him looking exhausted and ill.

An important element in this tremendous burden of work was Nijinsky's next ballet, *Jeux* (Games), to a score by Debussy (who incidentally hated the choreography of both this and *L'Après-Midi d'un faune*).

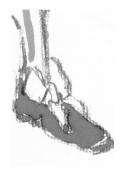

Design for the costume of a guest in the ballet
La Légende de Joseph

___

1914

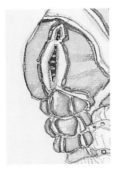

The costumes differed little from those to be seen at any sporting event of the period. The public could not understand Nijinsky's geometric movements and flat, abstract forms, and the ballet met with a poor reception.

This disappointing response, however, was to pale into insignificance beside the riot which broke out when his next ballet was first performed in Paris, on 29 May 1913. The violent reaction to *Le Sacre du Printemps* was prompted not just by the difficult, ungainly choreography but by

Design for the costume of two Negroes in the ballet
La Légende de Joseph

1914
32.5 x 41.3 cm
Sotheby's, Private collection

C. Bakst
1920

Stravinsky's driving rhythms and shattering harmonic tensions, which, nearly ninety years later, have lost none of their thrilling, visceral power. This and *Faune* marked a complete rupture with the traditional forms of the past. Bakst was not directly involved – the designs were by Roerich – but he was as enthusiastic as his colleagues about this seminal work, which is still so evocative of the Ballets Russes.

Set design for the backcloth in the ballet
The Sleeping Beauty

1916
66 x 52 cm
Evergreen House Foundation, Baltimore

209

The Grey Eminence 1914-1924

The last decade or so of Bakst's life was, for the most part, an anticlimax, artistically. His greatest achievements were behind him, his health was poor, and although he kept working as hard as ever, he only once more scaled the astonishing heights of the first Ballets Russes seasons. What he did do was to take his place as the "grand old man" of theatrical design.

Set design for the prologue of the ballet
The Sleeping Beauty

1916
84 x 72.5 cm
Evergreen House Foundation, Baltimore

He was much in demand as a lecturer and mentor, travelling far and wide to give the benefit of his experience and opinions of stage design in general. By 1914 it was becoming obvious that Diaghilev's company was in trouble. Box-office receipts were falling. The difficult new ballets by Nijinsky were too advanced for some audiences, but they had all seen *Firebird* and *Petrushka*, *Shéhérazade* and *Le Carnaval* – and there was nothing else coming along to tempt them back.

Design for the costume of Hubart as the Eastern Prince and his page in Act I of the ballet
The Sleeping Beauty

1916
48.3 x 33 cm
Evergreen House Foundation, Baltimore

Morale among the dancers was at a low ebb following the cataclysmic split between Diaghilev and Nijinsky. When Romola and Nijinsky celebrated their surprising marriage in 1913, they had not appreciated the effect it would have on the autocratic Diaghilev, whose concept of loyalty translated into the belief that he owned Nijinsky body and soul. Certainly Nijinsky was naïve enough to believe all would be well, and was flabbergasted to be summarily dismissed from the company on a paltry excuse.

Design for the costume of Aladdin in the ballet
The Sleeping Princess

1916

BAKST
1916

Diaghilev was bitterly hurt by what he saw as Nijinsky's defection, but when he calmed down he realised immediately that he needed a new choreographer. He found a young dancer, newly graduated, who had aspirations to produce ballets. Leonide Miassine – later Massine – quickly took Nijinsky's place, in every sense. Possessing nowhere near Nijinsky's level of genius as a dancer, he nonetheless matured into a fine character performer and an interesting ballet-maker.

Design for the costume of Felicita in the ballet
Les Femmes de bonne humeur

1917
Victoria & Albert Museum, London

Felicita

Bakst
1916

217

He will be remembered most for his portrayal of the shoemaker in the 1948 Powell and Pressburger film *The Red Shoes*.

Bakst, still unwell, forced himself to finish the costumes for *Papillons*, a slight piece to Schumann's music, a pale echo of *Le Carnaval*. Diaghilev drove him on relentlessly. Fired by enthusiasm for Richard Strauss's early operatic shockers *Salome* and *Electra*, the impresario had been in discussion with Strauss since 1912 over an idea for a ballet by Nijinsky on the biblical subject of Joseph.

Variation of a costume design for Vaslav Nijinsky in the ballet *Les Orientales*

1917
The McNay Museum, San Antonio

NIJINSKY

He found a set designer in the Spaniard José-Maria Sert, whose Polish wife Misia was to become one of his dearest friends. In a quandary over the choreography, he adopted an unfamiliar air of humility and with considerable difficulty persuaded Fokine to come back. The costumes for *La Légende de Joseph* were entrusted to Bakst, who turned for inspiration to his sketches of Veronese done in Venice some years before, adapting the cut and colours of the clothes,

Battista in the comedy *Les Femmes de bonne humeur*

1917
Watercolour on paper
Evergreen House Foundation, Baltimore

blending Oriental and Western styles in a dazzling whole. The palette of reds, greens, mauves and orange was underscored with black, enriched with gold ornament.

A triumphant public reception greeted the new work, and Massine, in the title role, received enthusiastic notices. The critical reaction was generally more muted. There was a growing undercurrent of feeling that so luxurious a décor was too dominant, and that the dancers were rather overwhelmed by it.

Set design for Act II, scene 5 of the ballet *Aladdin*

1919
21.1 x 29.5 cm
The Museum of Modern Art, New York

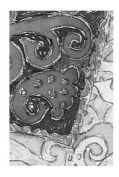

An irresistible move towards simplicity and away from opulence became discernible.

Bakst struggled on. He conceived a ballet on the subject of King Midas, not only writing the libretto but even working on the choreography. He had already begun work on the ballet *Orphée*, with music by Jean Roger-Ducasse, for a production at the Mariinsky Theatre when he fell seriously ill. The project was postponed for a year, but by then World War I had broken out and *Orphée*, like *Midas*, never saw the light of day.

Design for the costume of a Great Spaniard in the ballet *Aladdin*

1919
48.5 x 32.5 cm
Sotheby's, Private collection

Bakst
1918

225

The war had a profound effect on the fortunes of Diaghilev's company. They found themselves touring extensively – to the United States, to Spain, Portugal, and London – and Diaghilev had to move his headquarters to Switzerland. Bakst, whether out of conviction or trepidation, felt he could not take Nijinsky's part against Diaghilev in their quarrels. But he was often in dispute with the great man himself. Bakst was uncomfortably aware of Diaghilev's mercurial attitude towards him, and the realisation did nothing to chase away his depression, which grew steadily worse.

Russian Countrywoman

1920
Watercolour on paper, 68 x 49 cm
Private collection, Paris

In 1915, weak and miserable, he suffered a nervous breakdown and retired to a sanatorium in Switzerland for a few months.

A trip to Florence in 1916 to study the frescoes helped to restore some balance. By the following year, when the Ballets Russes was in Rome, he was ready to take up his watercolour palette again. Massine produced his first important ballet, *Les Femmes de bonne humeur* ("The Good-Humoured Ladies"), based on a play by the eighteenth-century Venetian dramatist Goldoni, and danced to an orchestration of some Scarlatti sonatas.

Design for the costume of the Wolf in Act III of the ballet *The Sleeping Princess*

1921
Watercolour, gouache, gold and silver on paper mounted on cardboard
Galleria de Levante, Milan

Bakst
1921

229

Bakst's sets appeared as if viewed through a magnifying glass, so that the lines of perspective were distorted. One critic, Sacheverell Sitwell, reported that there were already rumours about a rift between Bakst and Diaghilev, and that the costumes showed the effect of the artist's breakdown.

Bakst was keenly interested in new developments, and anxious to encourage young painters. He liked and bought the work of Henri "Le Douanier" Rousseau.

Costume for a Lady-in-Waiting in the ballet
The Sleeping Princess

1921
National Gallery of Australia, Canberra

His own work began to reflect his taste for Cubism, and he became friendly with Picasso, who painted him in 1922, and who was to design three fine sets for Diaghilev. Bakst also supported the young Italian painter Amedeo Modigliani, who has left a haunting portrait of him (1917), looking defensive and withdrawn.

Although he could see which way the wind was blowing, he was delighted to be given the opportunity to revive his early ballet *The Fairy Doll* in 1919.

Costume for a Lady-in-Waiting in the ballet
The Sleeping Princess

———————————

1921
Victoria & Albert Museum, London

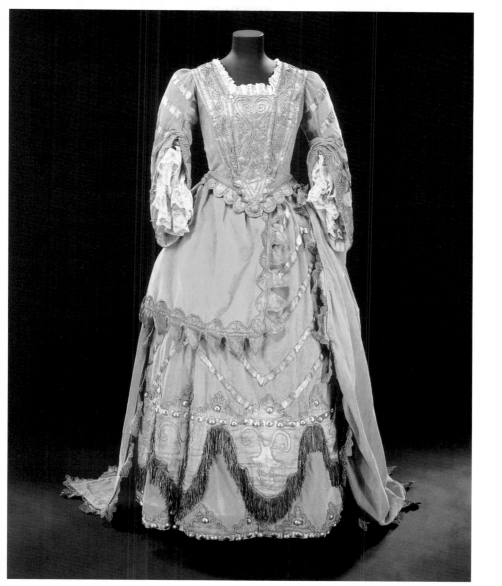

La Boutique fantasque (The Fantastic Toyshop), as the reworking was now known, was set to an orchestration by Respighi of some of Rossini's delectable little piano pieces, his "sins of old age". Massine did the choreography and also danced the can-can. Bakst made some amusing costume sketches, but was suddenly and high-handedly informed that the project was now being taken over by André Derain. Upset and deeply humiliated, Bakst immediately severed relations with Diaghilev.

Costume for the English Prince in the ballet
The Sleeping Princess

1921
Victoria & Albert Museum, London

He now entered a difficult phase, when his need to earn a living, as in his youth, was uppermost. Commissions did not come as thick and fast as before. For *Aladdin*, a spectacle at the Théâtre Marigny, Bakst simply reworked some of his costumes for *Shéhérazade* and harked back to exotic Orientalism for the set.

Diaghilev, too, was having a thin time. With no Nijinsky, no Massine (history had repeated itself when he fell in love with a girl and was abruptly dismissed), and no money coming in, he was desperate to revert to the successes of his pre-experimental days.

Costume for the Bluebird in the ballet
The Sleeping Princess

1921
Victoria & Albert Museum, London

A huge concept now began to take shape – Diaghilev was nothing if not capable of the grand gesture, even when times were hard. It was no less than the revival of the full-length *Sleeping Princess*, the grandest of Tchaikovsky's three ballets. Petipa had originally been responsible for it, and Diaghilev knew the décor had to underline the innately Russian quality of the music and the dancing. In 1921 he tempted Bakst with the proposal.

Portrait of Ida Rubinstein

1921
Watercolour, gouache and charcoal on paper mounted on canvas, 128.9 x 68.8 cm
The Metropolitan Museum of Art, New York

239

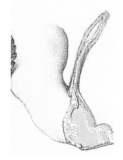

The whole enormous enterprise – five sets and over 300 costumes – constitutes Bakst's last great achievement. It was well received in London, where it had its première, but it was not in tune with the mood of the times and it was not enough to fill Diaghilev's coffers. The brief rapport between the two was not to last.

Bakst was a workaholic to the end. He was a member of several distinguished societies: the Salon d'Automne, the Société musicale française, and the Académie Royale in Brussels.

Judith Holding the Head of Holofernes after the ballet *Judith*

_____

1922
Oil on canvas, 46 x 53.5 cm
Sotheby's, Robert L. B. Tobin Collection, Marion Koogler McNay Art Museum, San Antonio

He published an essay, *Tchaikovsky and the Ballets Russes*. He worked on more theatrical projects: Stravinsky's *Mavra* and *Nuit Ensorcelée*, two further spectacles for Ida Rubinstein (*Artemis Toublée*, 1922 and *Ishtar*, 1924). He was widely revered – artists, actors, dancers, musicians, writers all looked up to him. His work was exhibited in Chicago, New York and Washington, and he spent a great deal of time in America lecturing and turning out decorative schemes for private clients.

Design for the costume of sultan Samarcande
after the ballet *Judith* (1909)

1922
Thyssen-Bornemisza Collection, Madrid

He died in Paris after several months of illness on 27 December 1924, at the early age of fifty-eight.

Although his talents as a painter and graphic artist are enough to ensure a place for him in the art firmament, it is his contribution to theatrical design that elevates him to one of the most brilliant of the stars. His impact in this field was incalculable. His colours, his undulating forms, the way "he visualised his costumes in motion, and poetic motion at that,"

Design for the costume of Mireille in the ballet
La Nuit ensorcelée

1923
45 x 29.2 cm
Sotheby's, Private collection

in the words of Arsène Alexandre, made him a unique theatrical phenomenon. The décor and costumes for his works – but above all, for *Shéhérazade, Le Spectre de la rose, Le Carnaval, L'Après-Midi d'un faune,* and *The Sleeping Princess* – have sunk into the consciousness of everyone who appreciates the theatre, so that every new production of these works must be weighed in the mind's eye against his incomparable creations.

Design for the costume of Ida Rubinstein in the title-role of Istar in the ballet *Ishtar*

1924
48.2 x 31.4 cm
Sotheby's, Private collection

"ISTAR

Mme I. RUBINSTEIN

Bakst

List of Illustrations

D